THE
TOTALLY PIZZA
COOKBOOK

D0469500

THE
TOTALLY
PIZZA
COOKBOOK

By Helene Siegel

Illustrated by
Carolyn Vibbert

CELESTIAL ARTS
BERKELEY, CALIFORNIA

Celestial Arts Publishing
P.O. Box 7123
Berkeley, CA 94707

Cover design and illustration: Bob Greisen
Interior design and typesetting: Susan Hernday
Interior illustrations: Carolyn Vibbert
Printed in Singapore
The Totally Pizza Cookbook is produced by becker&mayer!, Ltd.

Library of Congress Cataloging-in-Publication Data:
Siegel, Helene.

Totally Pizza Cookbook / by Helene Siegel.
p.   cm.
ISBN 0-89087-786-6
1. Pizza   I. Title.
TX770.P58S54   1996
641.8'24—dc20   95-48231
                                CIP

Other cookbooks in this series:
The Totally Eggplant Cookbook
The Totally Picnic Cookbook
The Totally Tomato Cookbook

WITH A TIP OF THE HAT TO MAVENS
ED LA DOU, WOLFGANG PUCK, AND
CALIFORNIA PIZZA KITCHEN—
ALL PIZZA TRAILBLAZERS.

CONTENTS

Serving Sizes

Most of the recipes are for individual, California-style 9-inch pizzas. They serve one person as a main course, or four or more as an appetizer. The simpler pies, especially those without cheese like the White Beans and Olives (page 80), can be cut into small pieces for wonderful hors d'oeuvres.

INTRODUCTION

W HEN IT COMES TO PIZZA, EVERYONE'S GOT AN OPINION.

Some swear by the New York variety: large, thin-crusted, topped with nothing more exotic than peppers or mushrooms, and eaten by the slice at a neighborhood joint called Sal's or Ray's.

Midwesterners, on the other hand, like it a few inches thick, baked in a pan to contain colossal quantities of meatballs and sausage, with a couple of pounds of cheese to ward off the cold.

And then there are the laid-back Left Coasters. This bunch likes to arrange things like duck meat and radicchio atop ever-so-thin crusts. They call this gourmet.

(Teenage boys, a small nation of pizza eaters unto themselves, seem to prefer any variety that requires a phone call and results in an unsightly stack of greasy cardboard boxes on kitchen counters. But that's another story.)

As an experienced pizza eater (and baker), I refuse to take sides. I prefer to keep an open mind and celebrate pizza in all its outrageous diversity, from humble bread, cheese, and tomato combinations to exotica like barbecued duck, marinated Thai shrimp, and, on occasion, even scrambled eggs and bacon.

The home is the best place for such wild experimentation. There are only two requirements regarding the making and serving of excellent pizza at home. Always serve it piping hot, right out of the oven, and skip the silverware. It tastes better that way.

Quick Tips

- *Have all the toppings ready before rolling out the dough.*
- *When trying out new combinations, do not get carried away. Three or four toppings usually work better than a huge pileup.*
- *Shred or grate cheeses for better melting, and always mix in some mozzarella for superior meltability.*
- *If eliminating tomato sauce, coat dough first with a thin layer of oil to prevent sticking.*
- *Adjust temperature to follow package instructions if using a prepared crust. Be sure to increase baking time to compensate for lower temperatures.*

HOMEMADE PIZZA DOUGH AND QUICK SAUCES

THE DOUGH

If you are new to bread baking, pizza dough is a great place to start. For very little effort the rewards are bountiful. Bread baking is never a precise science, as the ratio of water to flour varies according to climate and the condition of the flour. Just add the water gradually and use less or more according to the feel of the dough. When moist and slightly sticky, but not so tacky that it is difficult to work with, it's ready. To correct a dough that is too wet to handle, add flour a small handful at a time.

1 (^{1}/$_4$-ounce) package dry yeast
1 tablespoon sugar
1^1/$_2$ cups warm, but not hot, water
3^1/$_2$ cups all-purpose flour
^{1}/$_2$ cup semolina or cornmeal
1 tablespoon salt
3 tablespoons olive oil

BY HAND

Fill a measuring cup with $1/2$ cup warm water. Stir in the yeast and sugar. Let rest until foamy, about 5 minutes.

Combine flour, semolina or cornmeal, and salt in large mixing bowl. Stir in olive oil. Stir in the yeast mixture, and then slowly add remaining water until stiff and sticky. Turn onto lightly floured board and knead until smooth, moist, and elastic, about 10 minutes. Transfer to oiled bowl, cover with damp towel, and let rise in a warm place until doubled, 1 to 2 hours.

Punch down once or twice and turn out onto a lightly floured board. Cut into 6 pieces for individual pizzas. Gently knead each into ball. If baking soon, cover with towel and reserve on board. To store, wrap each tightly in plastic and store in refrigerator up to a day, or in the freezer for up to 2 months. Thaw in the refrigerator until soft.

BY FOOD PROCESSOR
(for large-size processor)

Combine the $1/2$ cup water, sugar, and yeast as in by hand method (see page 13).

In a processor fitted with plastic dough blade, combine flour, semolina or cornmeal, and salt. Pulse a few times to combine. Add the oil and briefly process.

With the machine running, add yeast mixture through the feed tube. Slowly pour in remaining water just until the dough clears the sides of the bowl and forms a ball on top of the blade. Process an additional minute. Remove and knead on floured board about 1 minute. Follow by hand instructions for rising.

BY ELECTRIC MIXER
(for heavy-duty mixer)

Combine the $\frac{1}{2}$ cup water, sugar, and yeast as for by hand method (see page 13).

In mixer bowl combine flour, semolina or cornmeal, salt, and olive oil. Mix with paddle to combine. Switch to dough hook and turn machine on slow. Pour in yeast mixture, and then slowly add remaining water until dough forms a ball around hook. Knead at medium speed about 5 minutes, until dough is smooth, moist, and elastic. Remove and follow by hand instructions for rising.

TO ROLL AND BAKE

Preheat the oven to 515 degrees F 30 minutes or longer with pizza stone or tiles on a medium-high rack.

Generously scatter cornmeal on pizza paddle to prevent sticking. On the paddle, flatten the dough ball with the palm of your hand and lightly dust the top with flour. Also dust the rolling pin.

Roll out the dough, from the center out, lifting and turning often, and adding more cornmeal as necessary. When dough is a 9-inch circle, lift, add additional cornmeal near the edge of paddle, and position dough as close as possible to the edge. Add toppings and place in the oven quickly to prevent sticking.

To place in oven, insert paddle, at slight upward angle, and with a quick back-and-forth motion slide the pizza onto the stone.

To remove, have a plate nearby and reach in with a long-handled spatula to transfer to plate. Long sleeves are a good idea for reaching into such a hot oven. Always let baking stone cool off in oven before removing.

Equipment
A pizza stone and a paddle make home pizza-making more fun. The hot surface of the stone, made of concrete or unglazed tiles, draws out moisture for a crisper crust. A long-handled wooden paddle or peel simplifies the tricky job of slipping pizza onto the hot stone. A stainless steel circular cutter is also useful to have.

WHOLE WHEAT HONEY DOUGH

1 (1/4-ounce) package dry yeast
1 1/2 tablespoons honey
1 1/2 cups warm, but not hot, water
1 3/4 cups all-purpose flour
2 cups whole wheat flour
1 tablespoon salt
2 tablespoons olive oil

Follow same method as for basic white dough (see page 12), substituting honey for sugar.

PARMESAN HERB DOUGH

½ cup grated Parmesan cheese
1 tablespoon chopped fresh rosemary,
   thyme, *or* oregano, *or* a combination

Add Parmesan and herbs with olive oil.
Reduce salt to 1 teaspoon.

---

*Subjecting this noble dish to a knife and fork is
sacrilege in the eyes of a Neapolitan, for pizza
cools and loses its singular flavor under the
torture of cutting.*
   —*Franco Galli in*
   The Il Fornaio Baking Book

CRISP CRACKER CRUST

Because of its higher ratio of water to flour, this dough is a little trickier to work with. Keep adding flour a bit at a time until the dough is manageable but still wet.

1 (¼-ounce) package dry yeast
2 teaspoons sugar
1²/₃ cups warm water
3½ cups all-purpose flour
¼ cup whole wheat flour
2 teaspoons salt
1 teaspoon freshly ground pepper
1 tablespoon olive oil

Stir together yeast, sugar, and water in large mixing bowl and let stand until foamy, about 10 minutes. Stir in remaining ingredients to make a soft, wet dough. Turn onto lightly floured board and knead until smooth and elastic, adding more flour a spoonful at a time if too sticky to handle. Transfer to oiled bowl, cover with towel, and let rise until doubled, about 1 hour. Follow basic instructions for rising (see page 13).

FOCACCIA

Rustic Italian flat breads can be made with pizza dough. They taste best hot from the oven.

> individual pizza dough balls (see page 12)
> olive oil
> salt
> Kalamata or other strong black olives, pitted

Lightly coat a 10-inch round cake pan with olive oil. Place risen dough ball in center and flatten by hand. Gently stretch until dough entirely covers bottom. Cover with towel and let rise 1 hour.

Preheat oven to 400 degrees F with pizza stone in place.

Remove towels and press dimples into dough with fingertips. Drizzle with oil, season with salt, and dot with olives. Bake until golden brown and crisp, about 35 minutes. Remove from pan and set on rack to cool slightly.

Pizza and focaccia represent a triumph of fantasia and strategy over a scarcity of ingredients, the instinct for survival transformed into an infinite variety of tastes.

—Carol Field in The Italian Baker

QUICK UNCOOKED
TOMATO SAUCE

A good prepared sauce is just fine for home pizza baking, but here is a quick make-it-yourself version for purists.

1 cup canned crushed Italian peeled tomatoes
1 tablespoon tomato paste
2 teaspoons dried crumbled oregano
salt and freshly ground pepper

Combine ingredients in a small bowl.

TRADITIONAL
PIZZAS

PLUM TOMATOES
AND MOZZARELLA

For pizza purists, nothing more than sliced
tomatoes, fresh herbs, and a sprinkling of cheese
is required.

1 (5-ounce) pizza dough ball (see page 12)
olive oil
2 plum tomatoes, sliced crosswise
1/2 cup shredded mozzarella cheese
1 garlic clove, thinly sliced
4 basil leaves, thinly sliced
1/4 cup grated Parmesan cheese

Preheat oven to 515 degrees F with pizza
stone in place.

Roll out dough on a cornmeal-coated paddle. Lightly coat with olive oil. Cover with single layer of tomato slices, leaving edges bare for crust. Sprinkle with mozzarella, garlic, basil, and Parmesan. Bake 8 to 10 minutes, until cheese is melted and bubbly.

Perfect Timing
Perfect pizza demands some vigilance. The key is to remove it from the oven as soon as the edges are charred, the bottom is dark and crisp, and the cheese is melted and runny but not burnt. A minute or two can make a big difference.

BIANCA

An all-white cheese pizza is a nice change.

1 (5-ounce) pizza dough ball (see page 12)
olive oil
$1/2$ cup shredded mozzarella cheese
$1/2$ cup shredded smoked Gouda cheese
$1/4$ cup grated Parmesan cheese
3 or 4 very thin slices onion
2 garlic cloves, thinly sliced
4 basil leaves, thinly sliced
$1/4$ cup crumbled soft goat cheese

Preheat oven to 515 degrees F with pizza stone in place.

Roll out dough on a cornmeal-coated paddle. Lightly coat with olive oil. Sprinkle on mozzarella, Gouda, and Parmesan, leaving edges bare. Top with onion rings, garlic, basil, and goat cheese. Bake 8 to 10 minutes.

FOUR SEASONS

Quatro Stagioni, heaped with artichokes
and mushrooms, is a personal favorite.

1 (5-ounce) pizza dough ball (see page 12)
3 tablespoons tomato sauce
3/4 cup shredded mozzarella cheese
1 thin slice prosciutto, torn in strips
2 marinated artichoke heart halves, cut in half
3 thinly sliced mushrooms
3 basil leaves, thinly sliced

Preheat oven to 515 degrees F with pizza
stone in place.

Roll out dough on cornmeal-coated
paddle. Coat with tomato sauce, leaving a
1-inch edge bare for crust. Sprinkle with
1/2 cup of cheese. Top with prosciutto, artichokes, mushrooms, and basil. Sprinkle with
remaining cheese. Bake 8 to 10 minutes.

NIÇOISE

In southern France, pizza has a thin crust,
charred edges, and the strong flavors of the region.

1 (5-ounce) pizza dough ball (see page 12)
6 tablespoons tomato sauce
1/4 teaspoon dried oregano
3/4 cup shredded mozzarella cheese
3 Kalamata olives, pitted and halved
1 garlic clove, thinly sliced
4 anchovies or 1 thin slice prosciutto,
   in 4 thin strips
1 teaspoon capers, drained

Preheat oven to 515 degrees F with pizza
stone in place.

Roll out dough on cornmeal-coated

paddle. Spread tomato sauce, leaving edges bare. Sprinkle with oregano and top with ½ cup mozzarella. Top with olives, garlic, anchovies or prosciutto, and capers. Sprinkle remaining cheese over top and bake 8 to 10 minutes.

Pizza Storage

Pizza dough balls can be wrapped well in plastic and stored in the refrigerator about a day or frozen for up to 2 months. Already-baked pizza can also be frozen. Let pizza cool and then wrap well. (Double-wrap in foil and zipper-lock freezer bag.) To defrost, bake in preheated 400-degree F oven for about 15 minutes.

ESCAROLE, OLIVES, AND GARLIC

Escarole, a slightly bitter salad green also known as chicory, was a staple in Italian-American immigrant homes.

1 (5-ounce) pizza dough ball (see page 12)
1 small head escarole, leaves separated, washed, and chopped
3 tablespoons olive oil
salt
4 garlic cloves, minced
5 Kalamata olives, pitted and halved
$1/4$ cup tomato sauce
$1/4$ cup cubed mozzarella cheese

Preheat oven to 515 degrees F with pizza stone in place.

Bring medium pan of water to
a boil and blanch escarole 1 minute.
Drain. Heat oil in medium saucepan over
medium-high heat. Cook escarole with salt,
garlic, and olives about 10 minutes.
Remove and drain excess liquid.

Roll out dough on cornmeal-coated paddle. Lightly coat with tomato sauce, leaving
edges bare. Top with generous layer of escarole and dot with mozzarella. Bake 8 to
10 minutes.

SAUSAGE AND ARUGULA

This hearty favorite comes from my neighborhood pizzeria, Farfalle.

1 (5-ounce) pizza dough ball (see page 12)
3 tablespoons tomato sauce
1/3 cup shredded mozzarella cheese
18 arugula leaves, stemmed and thinly sliced
1/2 pound sweet Italian sausage, casing removed
2 tablespoons grated Parmesan cheese
1 tablespoon chopped fresh basil

Preheat oven to 515 degrees F with pizza stone in place.

Roll out dough on cornmeal-coated paddle. Coat with tomato sauce, leaving edges bare. Sprinkle on mozzarella and top with arugula and sausage. Sprinkle with Parmesan and basil. Bake 8 to 10 minutes.

SAUSAGE, SPINACH, AND RICOTTA

Mild spinach and ricotta balance the strongly flavored sausage in this traditional pie.

1 (5-ounce) pizza dough ball (see page 12)
3 tablespoons tomato sauce
$1/4$ cup ricotta cheese
$1/3$ cup fresh spinach leaves, washed and chopped
$1/2$ pound sweet Italian sausage, casing removed
2 tablespoons grated Parmesan cheese

Preheat oven to 515 degrees F with pizza stone in place.

Roll out dough on cornmeal-coated paddle. Coat with tomato sauce, leaving edges bare. Spread the ricotta, leaving 1 inch of tomato sauce bare along edges. Sprinkle on spinach, sausage, and Parmesan. Bake 8 to 10 minutes.

ROASTED EGGPLANT AND FRESH TOMATOES

1 (5-ounce) pizza dough ball (see page 12)
1 Japanese eggplant, skin on, thinly sliced
   at an angle
olive oil
salt
$3/4$ cup shredded mozzarella cheese
2 tablespoons diced plum tomatoes
2 teaspoons pesto

Preheat oven to 450 degrees F. Arrange eggplant slices in single layer on oil-coated
baking tray. Sprinkle with salt and bake
until golden and soft, 5 minutes per side.

Turn heat up to 515 degrees F and place stone in oven.

Roll out dough on cornmeal-coated paddle. Lightly coat with oil. Cover with mozzarella and arrange eggplant in spoke pattern, leaving edges bare. Sprinkle with tomatoes and dot with pesto. Bake 8 to 10 minutes.

Ancient Pizza
The first recorded flat bread, the forerunner of modern pizza, was laganum. *This cracker-like bread, referred to by Virgil and Horace, was typically seasoned with garlic, parsley, coriander, or dry cheese.*

ROASTED POTATO
AND PROSCIUTTO

*Potatoes may not be a traditional topping, but
when they're paired with prosciutto the resulting
pie is convincingly Italian.*

1 (5-ounce) pizza dough ball (see page 12)
2 medium red potatoes with skins,
    thinly sliced
olive oil
salt
1 thin slice prosciutto, cut in strips
$1/4$ cup shredded mozzarella cheese
$1/4$ cup shredded fontina cheese

Preheat oven to 450 degrees F.
Coat a baking tray with oil and
arrange potato slices in single layer.
Sprinkle with salt and drizzle with oil.
Bake until soft and slightly golden,
7 minutes per side.

Turn heat up to 515 degrees F and place
pizza stone in oven. Roll out dough on
cornmeal-coated paddle. Lightly coat with
olive oil. Arrange prosciutto in single layer,
leaving edges bare. Top with potato slices in
single layer. Combine cheeses and sprinkle
over top. Bake 8 to 10 minutes.

INDIVIDUAL NEW YORKER

True New York pizza is meant to be eaten by the slice, standing up, at a place called Ray's. Here is a former New Yorker's pale (but good) imitation. Serve with red chile flakes for sprinkling and cold soda—expensive red wines are strictly forbidden.

1 (5-ounce) pizza dough ball (see page 12)
2 tablespoons tomato sauce
$^1/_2$ cup shredded mozzarella cheese
$^1/_4$ cup grated Parmesan cheese
$^1/_2$ green bell pepper, seeded and cut in strips
5 thin slices onion
6 slices pepperoni

Preheat oven to 515 degrees F with pizza stone in place.

Roll out dough on cornmeal-coated paddle. Coat with tomato sauce, leaving edges bare for crust. Combine cheeses and sprinkle $1/2$ cup over sauce. Top with pepper, onions, and pepperoni. Sprinkle with remaining cheese mix and bake 8 to 10 minutes.

MUSSELS MARINARA

Seafood is a traditional pizza topping in southern Italy and France.

1 (5-ounce) pizza dough ball (see page 12)
1 dozen mussels, scrubbed and debearded
2 cups white wine
2 tablespoons tomato sauce
3/4 cup shredded mozzarella cheese
5 or 6 slices, thinly shaved fennel bulb
4 Kalamata olives, pitted and halved
2 tablespoons chopped fresh basil

Preheat oven to 515 degrees F.

Bring wine to a boil in small saucepan. Add mussels, cover pot, and reduce to simmer. Cook until shells open, about 5 minutes. Remove with slotted spoon.

When cool enough to handle,
remove and discard shells.

Roll out dough on cornmeal-coated
paddle. Coat with tomato sauce, leaving
edges bare for crust. Sprinkle with ½ cup of
cheese. Top with fennel, olives, and mussels
in single layer. Sprinkle with basil and
remaining cheese, being careful to cover
mussels. Bake about 8 minutes.

---

*There exist a few things that are absolutely per-
fect. . . . There is no way to improve upon the
shape and function of the egg. Nor upon the
taste of genuine Neapolitan pizza.*

> —*Marcella Hazan in*
> More Classic Italian Cooking

CHICAGO STYLE

A great Italian-American contribution to pizza history, Chicago pizza is baked in a deep-dish pan—all the better to contain its abundant toppings. Apologies to any Chicagoans for this restrained, California version. Note: Half the dough recipe cut in half again will yield two 8-ounce dough balls.

olive oil
2 (8-ounce) pizza dough balls (see page 12)
$^{1}/_{2}$ pound hot Italian turkey sausage
1 cup shredded mozzarella cheese
$^{1}/_{2}$ cup shredded Parmesan cheese
$^{1}/_{2}$ cup tomato sauce
2 teaspoons dried crumbled oregano

Preheat oven to 500 degrees F. Lightly oil two 10-inch round cake pans.

Flatten pizza dough balls with palm of hand. Place in pans and gently stretch to edges, building up edges to contain filling. Cover and let rest.

Remove casings from sausage and fry meat in nonstick pan over medium heat until evenly browned. Drain.

Combine cheeses and divide in half. Scatter one quarter of the cheese mix over each pizza, leaving edges bare. Top each with cooked sausage and tomato sauce. Season with oregano and sprinkle with remaining cheese mix. Bake 15 minutes. Reduce heat to 400 and bake 10 minutes longer, until crusts are brown and cheese is bubbly and golden. Cool slightly and serve in pan.

SERVES 4 CALIFORNIANS

CALIFORNIA-STYLE PIZZAS

PESTO GOAT CHEESE

Though it may be possible to find pesto and goat cheese in Italy, to combine them and spread them on a pizza seems a truly West Coast thing to do. It is a delicious, rich combination.

1 (5-ounce) pizza dough ball (see page 12)
$^1/_2$ cup pesto
$^1/_4$ cup softened goat cheese

In small bowl, mix together pesto and goat cheese to make a paste. Preheat oven to 515 degrees F with pizza stone in place.

Roll out dough on cornmeal-coated paddle. Spread pesto mixture evenly over crust, leaving edges bare for crust. Build edges up slightly to catch drips. Bake 8 to 10 minutes.

BARBECUE CHICKEN LA DOU

I can't imagine anyone not loving this California standard after just one bite. It is a triumph of flavor over preconceptions.

4 (5-ounce) pizza dough balls (see page 12)
$1/2$ skinless, boneless chicken breast
1 cup sweet smoky barbecue sauce
2 cups shredded mozzarella cheese
1 cup shredded smoked Gouda cheese
$1/4$ cup fresh cilantro leaves
1 small red onion, thinly sliced

Cut chicken into thin strips and marinate in barbecue sauce 1 hour at room temperature. Preheat oven to 515 degrees F with pizza stone in place.

Roll out dough on cornmeal-coated paddle. Brush each with barbecue sauce, leaving a 1-inch edge bare for crust. Top with combination of mozzarella and Gouda cheese. Arrange the chicken in spoke pattern over cheese and sprinkle with cilantro. Top with onion rings and 2 or 3 tablespoons of cheese mix. Bake 8 to 10 minutes.

MAKES 4

ROASTED POTATO
AND SAUSAGE

1 (5-ounce) pizza dough ball (see page 12)
3 tablespoons tomato sauce
1 thinly sliced roasted red potato
  (see page 86)
$1/2$ cup shredded mozzarella cheese
$1/2$ cup grated Parmesan cheese
1 Italian turkey sausage, removed from casing

Preheat oven to 515 degrees F with pizza stone in place.

Roll out dough on cornmeal-coated paddle. Coat with tomato sauce, leaving a 1-inch edge bare for crust. Top with single layer of potatoes. Combine cheeses and sprinkle half over potatoes. Crumble sausage meat and add. Top with remaining cheese mix. Bake 8 to 10 minutes.

SANTA FE

This colorful pizza makes a great vegetarian meal.

1 (5-ounce) pizza dough ball (see page 12)
2 tablespoons tomato sauce
$1/2$ cup shredded mozzarella cheese
$1/4$ cup grated feta cheese
$1/4$ cup shredded cheddar cheese
$1/2$ roasted, peeled, seeded poblano pepper, diced
$1/4$ cup fresh corn kernels
1 tablespoon chopped fresh cilantro

Preheat oven to 515 degrees F.

Roll out dough on cornmeal-coated paddle. Coat with tomato sauce, leaving edges bare for crust. Mix the cheeses and scatter three-quarters over the sauce. Top with poblanos, corn, and cilantro. Sprinkle on remaining cheese. Bake 8 to 10 minutes.

CHICKEN WITH GARLIC AND ROSEMARY

It was love at first bite when I first tasted this sparkling combination at California Pizza Kitchen.

1 (5-ounce) pizza dough ball (see page 12)
$1/4$ boneless, skinless chicken breast
olive oil
1 tablespoon minced garlic
2 small rosemary sprigs
$1/2$ cup shredded mozzarella cheese
$1/2$ cup grated Parmesan cheese
1 tablespoon chopped fresh Italian parsley

Cut chicken into 1 x ¹/₂-inch strips
and place in small bowl. Add olive oil
to cover, garlic, and rosemary, and stir to
coat evenly. Cover with plastic and
marinate at room temperature 1 hour.

Meanwhile preheat oven to 515 degrees F.

Roll out dough on cornmeal-coated paddle.
Lightly brush with olive oil from marinade.
Sprinkle with half the mozzarella and
Parmesan. Top with chicken pieces in single
layer and sprinkle with parsley. Top with
remaining cheeses and bake 8 to 10 minutes.

SHRIMP AND FETA

The California version of Greek pizza.

1 (5-ounce) pizza dough ball (see page 12)
6 large shrimp, peeled, deveined,
 and halved lengthwise
olive oil
2 garlic cloves, minced
2 tablespoons tomato sauce
$^1/_3$ cup shredded mozzarella cheese
$^1/_3$ cup grated feta cheese
4 Kalamata olives, pitted and halved
2 scallions, white part only, thinly sliced

Place shrimp in small bowl. Pour in olive oil to cover, add garlic, and marinate at room temperature 15 minutes to 1 hour.

Preheat oven to 515 degrees F.

Roll out dough on cornmeal-coated paddle. Coat with tomato sauce, leaving edges bare for crust. Combine cheeses and sprinkle half over sauce. Lift out shrimp and place on pizza in single layer. Dot with olives and scallions, and sprinkle with remaining cheese. Bake 8 to 10 minutes.

BAY SCALLOP
AND ASPARAGUS

1 (5-ounce) pizza dough ball (see page 12)
3 asparagus spears, trimmed and cut
   in 1-inch lengths
salt
3 tablespoons tomato sauce
$3/4$ cup mozzarella cheese
$1/4$ cup grated Parmesan cheese
2 ounces bay scallops, washed and dried

Preheat oven to 515 degrees F. Blanch asparagus in salted boiling water until al dente, 3 to 5 minutes. Drain and rinse with cold water.

Roll out dough on cornmeal-coated paddle. Coat with tomato sauce, leaving edges bare for crust. Combine cheeses and sprinkle half on sauce. Scatter asparagus over top and arrange scallops in single layer. Top with remaining cheese mix, and bake 8 to 10 minutes.

The Italian Version

The word "pizza" derives from pizzicare—*meaning "pluck" or "pinch" in Old Italian and* picea—*the word for "pie" in Neapolitan dialect. Though other regions of Italy make flat breads, when the world orders pizza, they are looking for the Neapolitan version.*

The rise of pizza in Naples can be traced to the introduction of the tomato in the 16th century. By the 19th century, when mozzarella was introduced, pizza-making flourished. When King Umberto visited, a special pie was created by Raffaele Esposito of Pizzeria di Pietro, considered the best pizzaiola in Naples. It was red, green, and white, the Italian colors, and he named it for Queen Margherita.

MIDDLE EASTERN

Believe it or not, there is a precedent for pizza in the Middle Eastern kitchen. Lahmajun, *a dish of thin round bread topped with browned seasoned meat, is called Armenian pizza in Los Angeles-area Armenian restaurants. Note: The meat topping is enough for two pizzas.*

1 (5-ounce) pizza dough ball (see page 12)
1 tablespoon olive oil
3 tablespoons chopped onion
2 garlic cloves, minced
$1/2$ pound ground lamb
salt and freshly ground pepper
$1/8$ teaspoon ground cumin
pinch cinnamon
2 tablespoons tomato sauce
$1/2$ cup shredded smoked mozzarella
3 roasted eggplant slices
1 tablespoon chopped fresh mint

Preheat oven to 515 degrees F with pizza stone in place.

Heat olive oil in small skillet over low heat. Cook onion and garlic until soft. Add lamb, salt, pepper, cumin, and cinnamon, and turn heat to high. Sauté, stirring frequently until meat is evenly browned. Reduce heat to low and cook until pan is nearly dry, about 7 minutes.

Roll out dough on cornmeal-coated paddle. Lightly coat with tomato sauce, leaving edges bare for crust. Top with cheese, leaving some for topping. Spread on half the lamb mixture. Top with eggplant slices, mint, and remaining cheese. Bake 8 to 10 minutes.

FAJITA PIZZA

Only in America could a Californian lay claim to an Italian-Mexican pizza. Promise not to show this to any Italians, who have been known not to take such innovation lightly.

1 (5-ounce) pizza dough ball (see page 12)
3 ounces beef sirloin, cut into
    1 x $\frac{1}{2}$-inch slices
olive oil
$\frac{1}{4}$ teaspoon red chile flakes
2 tablespoons tomato sauce
$\frac{1}{2}$ cup shredded mozzarella
$\frac{1}{4}$ cup grated Parmesan cheese
$\frac{1}{2}$ green bell pepper, seeded and sliced
3 onion slices
2 tablespoons chopped fresh cilantro

Place beef in small bowl, pour in oil to cover, add chile flakes, and marinate at room temperature 15 minutes.

Preheat oven to 515 degrees F with pizza stone in place.

Roll out dough on cornmeal-coated paddle. Coat with tomato sauce, leaving edges bare for crust. Combine cheeses and sprinkle half over sauce. Top with peppers, onion, and beef in spoke pattern. Sprinkle with cilantro and remaining cheese. Bake 8 to 10 minutes.

CHINESE CHICKEN AND PEPPERS

A toasted bread crust replaces the rice in this light Asian meal.

1 (5-ounce) pizza dough ball (see page 12)
1/4 cup peanut oil
1 teaspoon sesame oil
1 teaspoon minced garlic
1 teaspoon minced fresh ginger
1/4 teaspoon red chile flakes
3 ounces chicken breast, cut into
    1 x 1/2-inch strips
soy sauce
3/4 cup shredded mozzarella cheese
1/4 red bell pepper, cubed
1/4 green bell pepper, cubed
3 slices onion
small handful bean sprouts

Combine peanut oil, sesame oil, garlic, ginger, and red chile flakes in small bowl. Add chicken, toss to coat evenly, and marinate at room temperature 30 minutes.

Preheat oven to 515 degrees F with pizza stone in place.

Roll out dough on cornmeal-coated paddle. Lightly brush with peanut oil and soy sauce. Scatter ½ cup of cheese, leaving edges bare for crust. Top with peppers and onion. Arrange chicken in single layer and top with remaining cheese. Bake 8 to 10 minutes. Remove and sprinkle with bean sprouts.

BARBECUED DUCK
AND LEEKS

Purchase burnished barbecued duck in take-out shops in Chinatown for instant gourmet dinners. French preserved duck or confit may be substituted, if more easily available. Just for the record: There is no tradition of cheese in China.

1 (5-ounce) pizza dough ball (see page 12)
2 tablespoons peanut oil
1 leek, white part only, cleaned, halved, and sliced
$\frac{1}{2}$ cup shredded smoked mozzarella cheese
$\frac{1}{4}$ cup grated Parmesan cheese
$\frac{1}{2}$ Chinese barbecued duck, skin and bone removed, and meat shredded
handful bean sprouts

Heat 1 tablespoon oil in small skillet over medium-low heat. Cook leeks until soft and set aside.

Preheat oven to 515 degrees F with pizza stone in place.

Roll out dough on cornmeal-coated paddle. Coat with remaining oil. Combine cheeses and sprinkle $1/2$ cup over dough, leaving edges bare. Top with leeks and duck, in single layer. Sprinkle with remaining cheese mix. Bake 8 to 10 minutes. Remove and sprinkle with bean sprouts.

BREAKFAST PIZZA

This wonderfully comforting morning dish was inspired by a favorite Los Angeles haunt, Hugo's in West Hollywood. For more spice, top with tomato salsa. For more savor, add crumbled cooked bacon before the eggs, as they do at the restaurant.

1 (5-ounce) pizza dough ball (see page 12)
2 tablespoons olive oil
2 eggs, beaten
salt and freshly ground pepper
1 cup shredded mozzarella cheese
$1/4$ cup shredded cheddar cheese
1 tablespoon chopped fresh Italian parsley

Heat 1 tablespoon oil in 8-inch skillet over high heat. Season the eggs with salt and pepper and pour into pan. Swirl to coat bottom and then reduce heat to low. Cook until bottom is set and top is still liquid, about 2 minutes. Set aside.

Preheat oven to 515 degrees F with pizza stone in place.

Roll out dough on cornmeal-coated paddle. Coat with remaining oil and sprinkle with half the cheeses, leaving edges bare. Bake about 5 minutes until dough is set and cheese melted. Carefully remove and transfer back to pizza paddle. Place unbroken eggs over cheese with spatula. Sprinkle with parsley and top with remaining cheese. Return to oven and bake 5 minutes longer, until edges are brown.

VEGETARIAN
PIZZAS

GARLIC AND HERBS

I like to cut this elegant garlic and herb bread into miniature wedges for nibbling with cocktails. It is particularly good made with whole wheat dough.

1 (5-ounce) pizza dough ball (see page 12)
2 tablespoons olive oil
2 garlic cloves, minced
1 tablespoon mixed chopped fresh
    rosemary, basil, and thyme
salt
$^1/_4$ cup shredded Parmesan cheese

Preheat oven to 515 degrees F with pizza stone in place.

Roll out dough on cornmeal-coated paddle. Brush with olive oil. Sprinkle with garlic, herbs, and a little salt. Sprinkle with cheese and bake 8 to 10 minutes.

ROASTED VEGETABLES

Leftover roasted vegetables—there is enough for two pizzas in this recipe—may be refrigerated and used in a few days.

1 (5-ounce) pizza dough ball (see page 12)
$1/2$ Japanese eggplant, with skin, thinly sliced at an angle
1 small zucchini, thinly sliced at an angle
$1/2$ red bell pepper, seeded and sliced
$1/2$ onion, thinly sliced
3 tablespoons olive oil
4 sprigs thyme
2 garlic cloves, peeled and crushed
3 tablespoons tomato sauce
$1/2$ cup shredded mozzarella cheese
$1/4$ cup shredded Gouda cheese

Preheat oven to 450 degrees F.
Combine eggplant, zucchini, red
pepper, and onion in a bowl. Add olive
oil, thyme, and garlic. Toss to coat evenly
and then place in single layer on baking
tray. Bake until soft and golden, about 15
minutes, turning once. Remove. Turn oven
up to 515 degrees F.

Roll out dough on cornmeal-coated
paddle. Coat with tomato sauce, leaving
edges bare. Combine cheeses and sprinkle
on half. Top with half vegetable mixture in
single layer and sprinkle with remaining
cheese. Bake 8 to 10 minutes.

ALL PEPPERS

For pepper aficionados—a smoky, rich, spicy mix of roasted peppers and cheese. (The pepper mix is enough for two pizzas.)

1 (5-ounce) pizza dough ball (see page 12)
1 red bell pepper
1 green bell pepper
1 poblano chile
2 tablespoons tomato sauce
$^1/_2$ cup shredded mozzarella cheese
$^1/_2$ cup shredded smoked Gouda cheese
1 tablespoon chopped fresh basil

Roast all the peppers on the stovetop or under the broiler until charred all over. Sweat in plastic bag 10 minutes. Peel, seed, and cut in thin strips. If preparing in advance, coat with a little oil, and store in covered container in refrigerator.

Preheat oven to 515 degrees F with pizza stone in place.

Roll out dough on cornmeal-coated paddle. Coat with tomato sauce, leaving edges bare for crust. Combine cheeses and sprinkle half on sauce. Top with half the pepper mix and basil. Sprinkle with remaining cheese. Bake 8 to 10 minutes.

The American Version
Like many transplanted foods, pizza got gargantuan, both in size and popularity, when it came to America. But it wasn't an overnight sensation. It first showed up in New York at the turn of the century, when Italian grocers and bakeries installed coal ovens in their shops. The first pizzeria was opened in 1905 by Gennaro Lombardi, on Spring Street in Little Italy.

WILD MUSHROOMS AND GARLIC

1 (5-ounce) pizza dough ball (see page 12)
2 tablespoons olive oil
4 garlic cloves, minced
4 ounces wild mushrooms such as shiitake
    caps, oyster, or chanterelles, thinly sliced
olive oil
1/2 cup shredded mozzarella cheese
1/4 cup crumbled soft goat cheese
2 tablespoons chopped fresh Italian parsley

Preheat oven to 515 degrees F with pizza stone in place.

Heat oil in small skillet over medium-high heat. Sauté garlic less than 1 minute and add mushrooms. Sauté about 2 minutes longer, just to soften.

Roll out dough on cornmeal-coated paddle. Lightly coat with olive oil. Combine cheeses and sprinkle half over oil. Top with cooked mushrooms, parsley, and remaining cheese mix. Bake 8 to 10 minutes.

GREAT CAESAR'S PIZZA

Here is everyone's favorite salad served on top of everyone's favorite bread product. It makes a nice first course for a casual dinner with friends.

2 (5-ounce) pizza dough balls (see page 12)
4 cups washed, dried, and sliced romaine
   lettuce
2 anchovies
1 garlic clove, peeled
3 tablespoons olive oil
$1/4$ cup grated Parmesan cheese
3 tablespoons red wine vinegar
Tabasco, Worcestershire, salt, and pepper
   to taste

Preheat oven to 515 degrees F with pizza stone in place. Chill lettuce.

Combine anchovies, garlic, oil, Parmesan, red wine vinegar, and seasonings to taste in blender. Purée to make dressing. Taste and adjust seasonings.

Roll out dough balls, one at a time, on cornmeal-coated paddle. Bake until crisp, about 8 minutes. Transfer to serving platters. Pour dressing over salad and toss well. Divide and place over baked crusts. Cut in wedges to serve.

MAKES 2

Il seems simple enough, but on closer inspection it is really very complicated. Pizza is made with oil, bacon, lard, cheese, tomato, or small fish. It is the yardstick by which the whole market is measured.

>   —*Alexandre Dumas in*
>   Grand Dictionnaire de la Cuisine

SMOKED MOZZARELLA AND RADICCHIO

Don't let the chic-sounding ingredients turn you away from this elegant combination. It is an utterly delicious blend of bitter and smoky flavors.

1 (5-ounce) pizza dough ball (see page 12)
2 tablespoons tomato sauce
$\frac{1}{2}$ cup shredded smoked mozzarella
$\frac{1}{2}$ cup grated Parmesan cheese
$\frac{1}{2}$ cup thinly sliced radicchio

Preheat oven to 515 degrees F with pizza stone in place.

Roll out dough on cornmeal-coated paddle. Lightly coat with tomato sauce. Combine cheeses and top with half. Sprinkle on radicchio and top with remaining cheese mix. Bake 8 to 10 minutes.

HOLD THE CHEESE, PLEASE

WHITE BEANS AND OLIVES

Peppery crisp cracker crust (page 20) is delicious
with this garlicky white bean pizza—a neat choice
for cocktails. Leftover bean dip may be refrigerated.

1 (5-ounce) pizza dough ball (see page 12)
1 (15-ounce) can cannelini *or* white beans
3 teaspoons minced garlic
1 tablespoon lemon juice
salt and freshly ground pepper
olive oil
1 teaspoon minced fresh thyme, rosemary,
    or parsley
5 Kalamata olives, pitted and halved
2 tablespoons chopped fresh Italian parsley

Drain and rinse beans. Combine in food processor or blender with 2 teaspoons garlic, lemon juice, salt, and pepper. Purée to make a paste. (Makes 1 cup)

Preheat oven to 515 degrees F with pizza stone in place.

Roll out dough on cornmeal-coated paddle. Lightly coat with olive oil, 1 teaspoon garlic, and minced thyme, rosemary, or parsley. Bake until crisp and brown, about 8 minutes. With spatula remove and return to paddle. Spread with half of bean paste, leaving edges bare, and scatter on olives and parsley. Carefully return to oven and bake 1 minute longer, just to heat through.

PESTO AND EGGPLANT

Though pesto does not quite qualify as cheeseless, this pizza does not have the richness of a traditional cheese pizza.

1 (5-ounce) pizza dough ball (see page 12)
1 Japanese eggplant, trimmed and thinly
    sliced on diagonal
olive oil
salt
6 tablespoons pesto
3 tablespoons diced plum tomatoes

Preheat oven to 450 degrees F. Arrange eggplant in single layer on oil-coated baking sheet. Sprinkle with salt, drizzle with oil, and roast until golden, about 7 minutes per side. Turn heat up to 515 degrees F and place baking stone in oven.

Roll out dough on cornmeal-coated paddle. Coat with pesto, leaving edges bare for crust. Top with single layer of eggplant, dot with tomatoes, and bake 8 to 10 minutes.

Pizza really took off after World War II, when returning soldiers sought to duplicate the foods they had experienced in Europe. When innovative New York pizzerias started selling pizza by the slice and moved the pizza-maker to the front window, where he could twirl the dough in the air, the pies really started to fly. In 1947, Chicago entrepreneurs Ike Sewall and Ric Riccardo of Pizzeria Uno tried to upstage New Yorkers with their deep-dish pizza, now the windy city's claim to pizza immortality.

CARAMELIZED ONION NIÇOISE

This traditional French onion pizza, known as pissaladiere, *is good served hot or at room temperature. It is also delicious made with a large, store-bought gourmet pizza crust.*

2 (5-ounce) pizza dough balls (see page 12)
$1/4$ cup olive oil
4 medium onions, thinly sliced
salt and freshly ground pepper
2 teaspoons chopped fresh thyme *or*
    1 teaspoon dried
8 anchovies
$1/4$ cup small black olives such as Niçoise
    or pichouline

Heat the oil in a large skillet over medium-low heat. Add onions, salt, pepper, and thyme. Cover and cook, stirring occasionally, until onions are wilted and beginning to brown, about 45 minutes.

Preheat oven to 515 degrees F with pizza stone in place.

Roll out dough, one at a time, on cornmeal-coated paddle. Coat with half onion mixture, leaving edges bare for crust. Arrange 4 anchovies over each in a spoke pattern and dot with olives. Bake 8 to 10 minutes.

ROASTED GARLIC POTATOES

For those who can't get too much of a good thing—an appetizer pizza slathered with roasted garlic paste and dotted with potatoes.

1 (5-ounce) pizza dough ball (see page 12)
2 heads garlic, tops trimmed
olive oil
1 small red potato, cut in ¼-inch cubes
salt and freshly ground pepper

Preheat oven to 500 degrees F. Place garlic in small roasting pan, drizzle with oil, and bake until softened and charred in spots, about 25 minutes. Let cool, then squeeze to peel. Mash garlic into paste with a fork, adding a spoon or two of olive oil, if dry. Turn oven up to 515 degrees F with stone in place.

Bring a small pot of water to a boil. Add potatoes and pinch of salt and cook 5 minutes. Drain, rinse with cold water, and drain.

Roll out dough on cornmeal-coated paddle. Lightly coat with olive oil. Spread on garlic paste, leaving edges bare for crust. Scatter potatoes over top, season with salt and pepper, and bake 8 to 10 minutes.

MARINATED TOMATOES WITH GARLIC

If you believe that simple is best when it comes to Italian food, try this elegant disk of dough topped with garlicky fresh tomatoes.

1 (5-ounce) pizza dough ball (see page 12)
2 large plum tomatoes, seeded and diced
3 tablespoons olive oil
2 garlic cloves, minced
salt and freshly ground pepper
1 tablespoon chopped fresh basil *or*
  1 teaspoon dried oregano

Combine tomatoes, olive oil, garlic,
salt, pepper, and basil or oregano
in small bowl. Marinate at room temperature 30 minutes to 3 hours.

Preheat oven to 515 degrees F
with pizza stone in place.

Roll out dough on cornmeal-coated
paddle. Arrange tomato mixture in circle,
leaving edges bare for crust. Place in oven,
reduce heat to 475 degrees F, and bake until
edges are dark brown, 15 minutes.

It wasn't until the 1960s that pizza took the giant leap from simple peasant food to big business with the growth of national pizza chains. Since then pizza has outpaced hot dogs and hamburgers as America's favorite snack food, resulting in fierce competition between the chains. Price wars, two-for-one deals, home delivery, and such innovations as cheese-stuffed pizza crust have been the result.

JUST DESSERTS

APPLE PIE PIZZA

Baked apples and pastry are a timeless combination. Frozen puff pastry, available in sheets at the supermarket, makes this elegant company dessert easy to make.

> 1 9-inch square sheet frozen puff pastry
> 2 tablespoons butter
> 2 tablespoons sugar
> 3 Granny Smith apples, peeled, cored, and
>   thinly sliced in wedges
> 1 teaspoon brandy or cognac
> 1 egg, beaten with 1 tablespoon cold water
> cinnamon for dusting

Preheat oven to 425 degrees F. Follow package directions for defrosting pastry, and place on board. (If using fresh pastry, roll out to ¼-inch thickness.) With sharp knife,

trim corners to create circle and
place on uncoated baking sheet. Prick
all over with fork and refrigerate.

Melt butter in skillet over medium heat.
Add sugar and apples and cook, stirring
frequently, until apples are softened but not
falling apart. Stir in brandy and remove
from heat. Transfer to bowl and refrigerate
15 minutes.

Remove pastry, and brush with egg wash.
Arrange apples and the liquid in pan in
center of pastry, leaving edges bare. Lightly
sprinkle with cinnamon. Transfer to oven
and bake until edges are brown and puffed,
about 25 minutes. Let sit 5 minutes, then
transfer with spatula to rack to cool.

SERVES 6

BROWNIE PIZZA

*In true pizza style, this basic brownie tart—
drizzled with white frosting, and sprinkled with
nuts—can be eaten out of hand without benefit
of knife, fork, or plate.*

4 ounces unsweetened chocolate, broken
1 stick plus 2 tablespoons butter
1½ cups sugar
4 eggs
2 teaspoons vanilla
1 cup all-purpose flour
1½ cups confectioners' sugar
about 2 tablespoons boiling water
½ cup assorted chopped nuts: walnuts,
   pecans, macadamias, and almonds for
   garnish

Preheat oven to 350 degrees F.

Combine chocolate and butter in medium-heavy saucepan and cook over low heat, stirring frequently, until melted and smooth. Pour into mixing bowl.

Add sugar and mix until smooth. Add eggs, one at a time, beating after each addition. Beat in vanilla. Add flour and gently mix until flour disappears. Pour into 12-inch tart pan with removable bottom or foil-lined pizza pan. Bake 25 to 30 minutes, until a toothpick comes out clean. Cool on a rack.

Make frosting by placing confectioners' sugar in mixing bowl. Bring water to a boil and slowly add to sugar, whisking constantly, just until thick enough to spread. Spread thin layer over pizza, leaving edges bare. Sprinkle on nuts and let set 10 minutes. Cut into wedges to serve.

SERVES 10

CONVERSIONS

LIQUID
    1 Tbsp = 15 ml
    $\frac{1}{2}$ cup = 4 fl oz = 125 ml
    1 cup = 8 fl oz = 250 ml

DRY
    $\frac{1}{4}$ cup = 4 Tbsp = 2 oz = 60 g
    1 cup = $\frac{1}{2}$ pound = 8 oz = 250 g

FLOUR
    $\frac{1}{2}$ cup = 60 g
    1 cup = 4 oz = 125 g

TEMPERATURE
    400° F = 200° C = gas mark 6
    375° F = 190° C = gas mark 5
    350° F = 175° C = gas mark 4

MISCELLANEOUS
    2 Tbsp butter = 1 oz = 30 g
    1 inch = 2.5 cm
    all-purpose flour = plain flour
    baking soda = bicarbonate of soda
    brown sugar = demerara sugar
    confectioners' sugar = icing sugar
    heavy cream = double cream
    molasses = black treacle
    raisins = sultanas
    rolled oats = oat flakes
    semisweet chocolate = plain chocolate
    sugar = caster sugar